JJ Waller's
Brighton
Pride

Introduction

"Brighton Pride is one of the most important events in the city, and in this book JJ Waller brilliantly captures its spirit."
Caroline Lucas MP

No other annual Brighton & Hove event can match the sheer scale and importance of Pride.

The huge parade in particular never disappoints and as it evolves, it inspires.

Looking back to Pride's tentative pioneering early years as 'a tea party in a park', when even just the simple act of being on the streets demonstrating 'under a rainbow banner' could invite derision, prejudice and hatred, we now realise how courageous those early campaigners were. They stepped out together sharing a strength of spirit and outrage that became the seeds to an event that has grown to embody the celebration of diversity that is fundamental to our city.

For a photographer Pride throws up many opportunities, and challenges. As ever, my goal is to transcend the cliché but that's not to say there are no pictures of Drag Queens in this book, far from it. Hopefully the pictures convey the sheer positivity of Pride not only for the parade participants but for the townsfolk that come out to admire and cheer the parade in their tens of thousands. What could be more joyous than seeing kids waving rainbow flags, or hearing the genuine cheers and applause of the crowd for the police and emergency services parading with Pride?

Even though Pride generates significant profits that support local social initiatives and charities, modern day Pride is not without its critics, many of whom think it has moved too far from its protest roots and feel it has been 'pink-washed' and 'homocapitalised'.

At the same time it is a testament to the distance travelled of the journey from a protest by some to a celebration by many and the inclusion that this signifies.

I have chosen to include along with my photographs a spectrum of Vox Pop quotes throughout the book that reflect the polarity of many of the opinions on both sides.

Who knows, maybe a future Pride will have a smaller, quieter alcohol free celebration in a neighbourhood park on Pride weekend?

Whatever happens I will be there taking photographs and enjoying the event with a playful curiosity, hugely proud of my city whilst carrying deeply held thoughts and respect for those who suffered and those who still suffer at the coal face of prejudice and bigotry.

The very word Pride is supercharged with meaning, put it together with the name of our city and you have an event as important as it is magnificent.

JJ Waller, June 2019

"My generation had to hide who and what we were. In my case, my wife married me and so helped me hide my true sexuality. I went to my first Brighton Pride parade more than ten years ago because I felt ashamed that I had always hidden the fact I was gay. Pride does more than anything else to further the acceptance of homosexuality and the understanding of just how many of us there are."
George Montague, 96, a campaigner for Turing's Law, which has seen thousands of gay men, including George, pardoned for historic offences committed under legislation that outlawed homosexual acts. George marches every year at Pride under the banner of 'The Oldest Gay in the Village'.

I love the way how freedom of being and expression is so often conveyed passionately through costume and clothing at Pride, mingling personal stories with social and political statements.
Vania Mills - Costumier

Pride day is our opportunity to show we are positive about who we are, but we should live in a world that enables feeling positive every day everywhere. Simeon Elliot - Urban Shepherd

The atmosphere is electric. I took my seven-month-old daughter on the parade last year and she loved it! So much fun and positivity. Tim Holtam - Brighton Table Tennis Club

The saviours of the city are the refuse collectors around Pride. Daniel Harris - Campaigner

Nobody should have to justify (to anyone) who they love and why. Pride's an unashamedly, no holds barred, flamboyant knees up... Visibility matters. Sarah Hutchings - Director, City Reads, Brighton

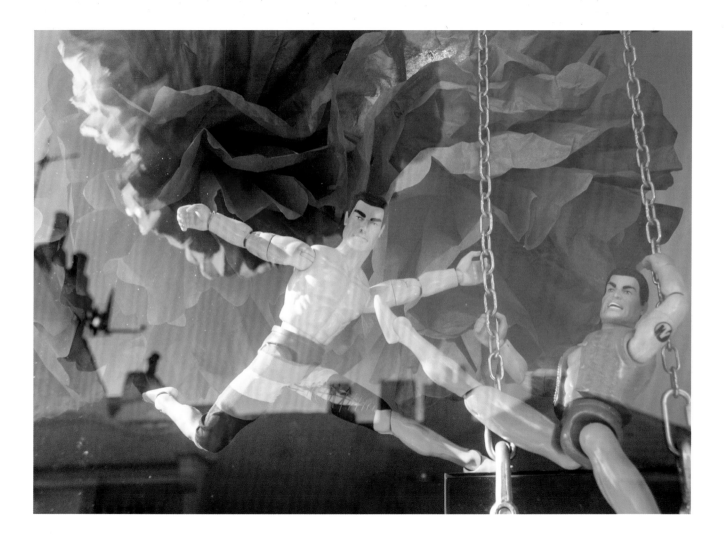

For me Pride is a time to remember those that fought for our freedom and to remember those who are still oppressed; the fight goes on... Miss Jason - Cabaret Artist

A celebratory bedazzling protest - politics as party - a time to parade our pride.
Stephen Wrench - Football correspondent

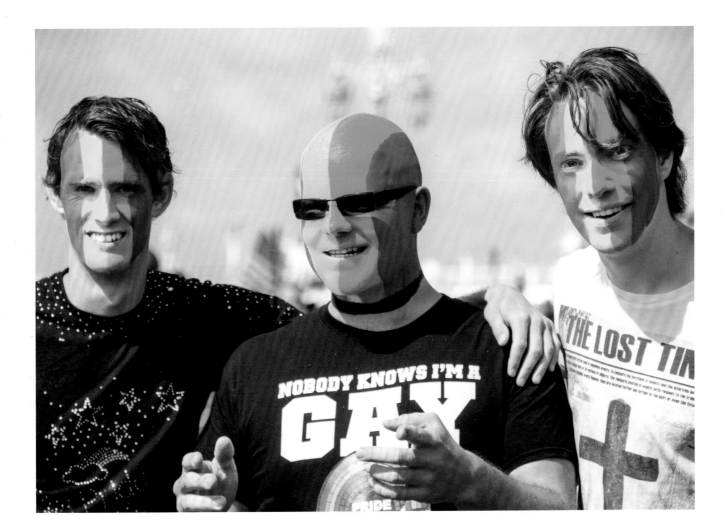

A genuine platform for promoting equality, diversity and inclusion that gives everyone involved (not just the LGBT community) the chance to show their support in a great party atmosphere.
Bob Cook - Brighton & Hove Buses LGBT+ Group

Text within the image:

Marielle Franco
- Brazilian Politician
- Human Rights Activist & Feminist
- Assassinated March 2018
- Bisexual, wife & mother

#WeAreProud

MERMA LIFE

Pride offers hope and solidarity to the whole LGBTQ+ community, and in particular to those who live in countries that continue to persecute people because of their sexuality or gender identity.
Hilary Cooke - Children's Literature Producer, Brighton Festival

Last year was my first time at Brighton Pride and as a gay man there are few places where I have ever felt so completely comfortable, accepted and welcome. Jake Turnbull - Blogger

Is it a celebration of Pride or just going to see Kylie and Britney? SB - Facebook

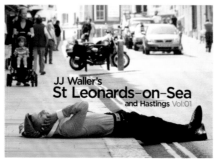

Credits

Special thanks to:

Jasmine Uddin

Victoria Doyle

Nione Meakin

Design: Alex Bamford

Print: Gemini - Shoreham

Published by Curious-Publishing

ISBN 978-09574390-6-1

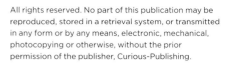